Deactivate Your

SURVIVAL TRANCES

Three Ways to Restore Your Life
After Trauma

Shuna Morelli

Book 3 of the BodyMind Bridge Series

BODYMIND
—BRIDGE—

Paperback ISBN: 979-8-9865334-0-7
eBook ISBN: 979-8-9865334-1-4
Audiobook ISBN: 979-8-9865334-2-1
First paperback edition September 2022

Cover Art: Gillian Hanington
Cover Design: Onur Aksoy
Layout and Interior Design: Heidi Flemons
Author's Portrait: Rebecca Ellison
Book Doula: Julie Barrett

Map of the Mind: Neurofeedback Alliance, *Understanding Brain Waves*

BodyMind Bridge Institute
Steilacoom, WA, USA
Shunamorelli.com

CONTENTS

FOREWORD

When I consider the content that has made the most profound impact on my life in recent years, I think of the gentle, clear, practical wisdom of Shuna Morelli and her BodyMind Bridge method of self-healing.

I grew up in an alcoholic home where severe, untreated mental illness was also present. This environment left me with coping mechanisms and survival skills that did just that—they helped me to cope and survive. But don't we all want more from our lives than to just survive?

I have sought healing in every aspect of my life for decades. Along my journey, I've learned many healing modalities, including cognitive behavioral therapy, 12-step recovery for codependency, emotional transformative therapy, meditation, and a deep relationship with God. These tools and practices have helped me navigate my mental, emotional, relational, and spiritual dis-ease. I've also called upon skilled practitioners of acupuncture, chiropractic care, and medical massage to treat the trauma and stress stored in my body, manifested as migraines, muscle spasms, and nerve pain. I vigilantly used all of these modalities and experienced such emotional freedom that I knew I had to share my healing with others.

In my work as a life coach and recovery mentor, I must say that all these modalities have served my clients well, and yet each tool and practice seemed a bit disjointed from the rest.

Enter Shuna and her BodyMind Bridge method of self-healing. Shuna's work, including this powerful little book you hold in your hands, has beautifully integrated every bit of healing work I've done thus far. And more than that, Shuna's work has helped me integrate each part of my true self—all the parts and pieces that were previously fragmented by trauma are being gently called back home.

This book serves as a beautiful reminder that my coping mechanisms from childhood helped me survive and served me well for a time, but now I have outgrown them. I can see younger versions of myself through the lens of love and empathy. Most importantly, I've learned how to connect with my younger, hurting self and give her what she needs to heal and feel safe. I can invite her out of the shadows and into the light where we can thrive together.

Deactivate Your Survival Trances has an immense amount of practical wisdom packed into its pages—wisdom that has guided me to a place of greater self-compassion. That is my hope for you as you read this book, and I'm confident it is hope well-placed.

May you know that you are worthy to receive the fullness of grace, compassion, wisdom, empowerment, and healing contained in these pages.

Heidi Le
Author, *Confessions of the Broken: A Codependent Rock Chick's Journey from Hopelessness to Healing*
Founder, Emotional Freedom Masterclass
Certified BodyMind Bridge Practitioner

INTRODUCTION

HERE'S WHAT YOU CAN EXPECT FROM THIS BOOK

I wrote this book so the average person who is burdened with trauma can know that this option for healing exists. You likely function well enough in the world as a capable adult, yet there is a battle hidden in you that continues to plague your general happiness. It's also likely you have kept those emotions buried as best you could. Yet, if your own 3-year-old child ran to you crying and afraid, you wouldn't send them away. You'd scoop them up, dry their tears, and hear their story. Then you'd help them know they are safe. What if you could do this with the younger selves inside you who are still crying and afraid?

This book will show you how to do this. If your trauma happened when you were 2, 12, or 20, and if you didn't get to vent the emotion out of the body, it is still in you. In your body. Your challenge is to do a search and rescue mission to help the fear finish its trajectory out of the body. Doing this inner work produces tangible results that you sense in your day-to-day life.

Many books teach about trauma so you can understand it better, but few reveal ways you can do something about it. This book does both.

The method I've developed to do this inner work is named BodyMind Bridge. I've guided hundreds of people into the deep healing part of their minds where they locate and then care for a younger part of themselves that is still hurting. Even though each person brings their own story, their own flavor of trauma, I've noticed some similarities:

- We all have trauma in us—some mild and some debilitating.
- It still affects us today.
- We don't realize we can release it and restore our life.

To this day, I marvel at what the average person can do when guided inward and shown how to shift and release the impact that past events have had on their life.

Part One explains what a survival trance is, a Map of the Mind so you know how your mind operates, and a few stories from people who have shifted and transformed their survival trances using the methods in part two of the book.

Part Two gets right to the goodies—how to deactivate the trauma in you. I offer three ways to do this, and each depends on how long ago it happened. Did your trauma just happen? Then refer to Chapter 4. Did it happen weeks or months ago? Flip to Chapter 6. Did it happen years or decades ago? Chapter 7 is waiting to guide you on your inner search and rescue.

> My caveat: If your trauma was ongoing and horrendous, or if you have been diagnosed with any type of psychosis, I ask you to first consult with your mental health professional before attempting the methods offered here. You must have a healthy attachment to reality to safely do this inner work. Personally, I believe most of our mental

health symptoms began with emotional trauma. Therein lies the challenge, and the hope.

Please don't minimize what you went through. It's likely your experience moved part of you into a survival trance. You'll learn in the first chapter that a survival trance helps get you through the traumatic moments, but if you carry it with you into adulthood, it becomes a burden that stays indefinitely. It's waiting for your permission to leave.

Here's the good news; it doesn't matter if the incident happened a few hours ago or months or years ago—there are ways to heal this inner wound. Let's not slap another Band-Aid on it, let's transform it.

⟶⟫⟩ ⟡ ⟨⟪⟵

I dedicate this book to you, dear reader—a regular human burdened by difficult life events! In my heart of hearts, I just want to say, you have all that is needed to heal the root cause of your trauma!

Blessings on your journey,

Shuna
Founder, BodyMind Bridge Institute
Shunamorelli.com

PART ONE:

THE BACKSTORY OF SURVIVAL TRANCES

"Human beings are born with an innate capacity to triumph over trauma. I believe not only that trauma is curable, but that the healing process can be a catalyst for profound awakening—a portal opening to emotional and genuine spiritual transformation."

—*Peter A. Levine*

WHAT IS A SURVIVAL TRANCE?

"All these years I thought there was no way to get over my past,
no way to get free of it. I was wrong."
—Stacey L., BodyMind Bridge client

IT HAPPENED TO ME

The first time I heard of a "survival trance," I was reading Stephen Wolinsky's pioneering book, *Trances People Live.* There was something about the concept of being in a trance that felt vaguely familiar to me. It made sense that when we are young and in danger, we store that fear in our bodies, but it wasn't until a traumatic memory of my own reared up from the depths that I truly understood the force and fury of this trance.

A song from my high school years triggered emotions I hadn't felt for decades. Within seconds, my skin flushed, and my heart hammered in my ears. In my mind's eye, I saw and heard and felt again a thing that happened when I was 15.

My dad had me pinned against the basement wall, his red face inches away as he screamed things at me that I don't even remember. Something about my friends and how dare I hang out with "people like that." He wasn't a drinker. He was a rager. He either sulked or threw things. The floors of our house were littered with eggshells, so we all got pretty good at staying in line. But something about me stepping out with friends who could take me away for the night, something about me feeling a teenage freedom, set him off. In that dank basement, his breath and spit showered my face. I could not run. I could not fight. So, I froze. My racing mind thought he might kill me. Any sense of personal power was erased, and I went numb.

This terrified 15-year-old part of me who surfaced in my awareness that day, in her ripped jeans and ponytail, had been 50 years mute, hiding in the shadows of my psyche, clutching her secret for decades. She appeared in my mind's eye like an apparition—still pinned against that basement wall. Somehow, I knew she was signaling that she wanted out. Out of the basement, out of the fear. She needed to feel safe. On that day, my nervous system activated a survival trance to keep me alive. My face went blank, my eyes vacant, and my dad saw. He stopped the assault and walked out.

Psychology calls these younger parts sub-personalities. The idea that we automatically go into a survival trance to get through moments like this gave me a glimmer of hope. It was now up to me to get her to safety. I just had to find out how.

*A survival trance comes to our rescue
when we are in danger and cannot fight or run.
Instead, we freeze.
We move our awareness away from the scene
to get through the experience and survive.*

WE HAVE A PERSONAL 911 CALL CENTER

We have a 911 call center in us that jumps into action when needed. Our nervous system collaborates with the endocrine system and together they initiate a survival trance that helps us stay alive until the danger has passed. This protective trance is meant to be temporary, but if we don't express it out of our body—if we keep it a secret—the trance can stay in us and cloud our vitality for the rest of our lives.

The word "trance" is a therapeutic term that describes when our awareness is in our deeper mind—the same territory familiar to people who meditate or who engage in contemplative prayer. But many practiced meditators don't realize they can make genuine inner changes while they meditate—changes that support their life and create more freedom in their outer world —freedom that is physically and emotionally tangible.

In chapter two, you'll find a Map of the Mind to help you better understand the outer and inner mind. It identifies the region of your mind—easily tapped into—that is encoded to self-heal.

IS SURVIVAL TRANCE A COMMON EXPERIENCE?

Living with one or more survival trances is very common. Seven billion people are on this planet, and all of us have experienced trauma—some big, some small. Don't be fooled into thinking the only people who live with trauma are soldiers in combat or victims of horrific violence. There are more ordinary events that can lead to trauma, and the list is long. Examples include: falling off your bike and breaking a bone, being bullied or gaslighted or continually ignored. Surgeries. Neglect. Car crashes. Social embarrassment. Natural disasters. Working in the emergency room or as a first responder. Kids enslaved as caretakers of a drug-addicted parent develop trauma. And one example of trauma few recognize is simply being a witness of violence.

Survival trance helps us in all these situations. As the event is unfolding, the survival trance kicks in and gets us through the brutal and disheartening moments in our lives. But it doesn't have to settle in and take root. If you can express the fear in that moment—yell or tell or run or fight—you can release the trauma energies from your body and the trance will dissipate. If you cannot express the emotion out of your body, that emotion will stay with you and continue to do its job. It will shield you from something that happened in your history, still on duty for something that is no longer relevant.

When we cannot speak about what happened,
or are too numb to even name it,
the survival trance will simply wait for you to help it leave.

This is where the good news enters. Since your nervous system had the ability to *activate* the survival trance, it follows that you can also *deactivate* the same trance even if it was initiated decades ago. This is not done by someone else or with medication. This is done by *you*.

WIRED TO HEAL

There is a powerful part of your inner mind that is neurologically wired to heal your symptoms at their source. You can lighten the grip of depression or anxiety with this part of your mind or discover and release the origin of chronic physical pain that the MRI cannot detect. You can even release the emotional grip your personal history still has on you. Learning to move your awareness into the quiet, restorative level of your mind—just below your conscious awareness—is the ticket.

These abilities may seem miraculous, but you were born with them. You entered the world in a body saturated with mind and spirit. Every cell is conscious. This mind and spirit housed in your physical form is *on your side* and wants the same thing you do. It is waiting for you to form an alliance with your deeper mind, so you can heal.

--->>> ✣ <<<---

You entered the world in a body saturated with mind and spirit.

--->>> ✣ <<<---

IF YOU CAN'T RUN OR FIGHT, YOU FREEZE

Survival trance is linked with the familiar fight, flight or freeze response built into our physiology. The third option—freeze—

happens when our bodies and minds are in deep peril. When we cannot fight back or run away, our last chance for survival is to freeze.

In his book *Waking the Tiger*, Peter Levine talks about the life-changing drama he witnessed when on an African safari. From the back of their Land Rover, the tour group watched a cheetah chase and capture a young impala. They followed the drama with binoculars and spotting scopes as the high-speed predator got closer and closer to the wild-eyed impala, swiped its hind end, and sent it tumbling in the dust.

The victorious cheetah sank its teeth into its victim's neck. The impala went limp and collapsed. Thinking it had finished the kill, the cat hauled its meal into the bush, covered it with leaves and walked away, apparently planning to eat it later.

Several moments went by, and everyone watching was startled to see the pile of leaves begin to move. Slowly, the injured animal stood, wobbly and shaken.

What happened next became the moment when Peter suddenly understood the mechanics of trauma held in the body. The little impala suddenly leaped high into the air and violently shook its entire body. It did this several more times, its chest heaving, its eyes rolled back. Then, the animal slowly quieted. Now stabilized, it calmly joined the nearby herd as if nothing had happened.

This animal knew instinctively to shake the trauma out of its body. Just moments earlier it was running hard for its life—adrenaline was dumping into its bloodstream, all survival systems on high alert. When it could no longer run, it activated its last chance to survive. It froze and collapsed.

Humans default to the same survival methods. When our bodies are on high alert, our nervous systems flip a switch and catapult us into our fight, flight, or freeze mode. Whether we're 4 or 40, when we cannot run and cannot fight back, we freeze—banking on the possibility that the danger will pass. In other words, we put ourselves in a trance—a survival trance. We remove our awareness from the scene and hope for the best. We dissociate so we can live another day. This is the strategy the little impala used to stay alive.

Why, then, do animals fare better after trauma than humans?

Animals instinctively shake the trauma from their bones, and this activity releases the excess adrenaline and survival energy pent up in their bodies. Animals don't have a voice in their heads that stops them from doing this self-rescue. They don't say to themselves, "What will the others think if I shake and scream and tremble right now?"

Many humans *do* have that voice in their head. If others are watching, we fumble to get back in control and override our instinct to let the body shake. We divert attention away from the part of the brain still in full alarm. Our pride and ego step in. We do all we can to regain our dignity.

If your body has ever shaken and trembled uncontrollably after a scare, maybe you thought something was wrong. That full body shaking is essential to reset your nervous system and regain equilibrium. When we don't shake the fear and excess adrenaline out of our systems, we stay in the trance. If we ignore our body's demand to shake it off, we leave behind a frightened younger part of us as the rest of us continues to adulthood.

In chapter three are several stories about regular people who deactivated their survival trances by following the methods in this book. Their stories will help you better understand how your survival trance(s) once served you and how they likely still inhibit you today.

YOUR DEFENDER AND HERO—THE HPA AXIS

The Hypothalamic-Pituitary-Adrenal axis (HPA) is the mechanism in our body that rockets us into the emergency fight, flight, or freeze response. When in danger, the nervous system and endocrine system team up to give us the best possible chance to live another day.

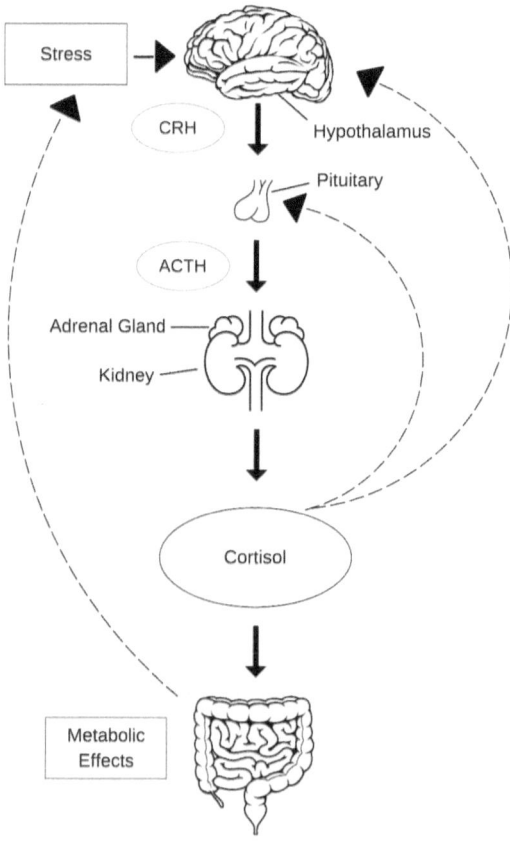

This HPA axis is a feedback loop that recruits a series of powerful glands to prepare your body and mind for survival.

Your hypothalamus is the first to activate. In your body's rush to protect you, the hypothalamus triggers a series of neural signals that cause the adrenal glands to dump adrenaline directly into your bloodstream. Adrenaline amps you into a state of hyper-arousal and you become practically superhuman. Pupils dilate. Respiratory rate skyrockets. Heart pumps more blood to muscles in the limbs. You can now lift a tractor.

Everything you need to run or fight is supplied. When you run hard or fight with all you've got, you use up excess adrenaline. This brings you back to a resting state. But if you freeze, you don't get to use up the flood of adrenaline, and your body and mind remain in a state of hyper-arousal.

Surprisingly, your HPA axis will kick in whether the danger is real or imagined. The danger can be as real as your car skidding out of control in a snowstorm, or as imagined as a flashback about abuse that happened long ago. Your body responds to whatever you decide is real.

⤞⟩⟩ ✻ ⟨⟨⟨⤝

Our symptoms have one purpose.
To alert us to the unattended trauma
still dumping adrenalin into our veins.

⤞⟩⟩ ✻ ⟨⟨⟨⤝

Anyone who still suffers from trauma will tell you they can't shake the feeling that it's still happening to them. They understand in their thinking mind that they are safe now, but the survival trance that once helped them stay alive tells them they are still in danger.

They feel this because their HPA axis is jammed, and they live in a constant state of hypervigilance. In the presence of a long-term stressor—either real or imagined—the HPA axis is constantly engaged because the stressor is still very real and present in the individual's mind.

Unable to switch off and recover, this constant anxiety will eventually morph into chronic emotional, mental, and physical symptoms. These symptoms have one purpose: to alert us to the unattended trauma that is still dumping adrenalin into our veins. The younger self who initiated the survival trance is begging you to complete the trajectory and get the trapped energy out of your body.

POST-TRAUMATIC STRESS: DISORDER OR INJURY?

When trauma keeps us hypervigilant, on edge, and unable to focus, it can lead to a diagnosis of post-traumatic stress disorder. But recent research suggests that not everyone with post-traumatic stress needs to be diagnosed with a disorder. Since it is an *injury* to the nervous system, it can often heal. *Depending on the severity of the trauma, the type of care available, and the participation of the patient, this injury can be temporary.*

If you are diagnosed with a disorder, it can feel like a life sentence. But an injury can heal.

SARAH

Thirteen-year-old Sarah was sprawled on her bed, listening to music. She heard a siren screaming down her street, and it stopped in front of her house.

She looked out the window. Her dad was motionless on the front lawn, his limbs arranged in horrific surrender. She ran out the door, gulping her fear, voiceless. Outside in the bright Texas sun, two paramedics were pumping her dad's stomach.

"What did he swallow?" A medic yelled.

"It must be these," her mom held an empty pill bottle. Sarah recognized it.

Her mind went stone silent, and she froze. Nothing made sense. Her dad had swallowed a whole bottle of anti-depressants.

Her senses slammed shut. She couldn't steady herself, had nobody to hold on to. In that moment, Sarah's nervous system came to her rescue and initiated a survival trance. It carried her away from the disturbance and moved her to an internal place of safety. Her body instinctively went into a survival trance to get her through the moment.

In slow motion, neighbors trotted toward the flashing lights, hands over their mouths. If they had looked at Sarah, they would have seen she had "checked out" as her traumatized nervous system carried her awareness to a faraway place.

Sara's story is one example of what can happen when our beautiful mind cannot process a traumatic experience. When we are in danger, we hide inside the trance. If at some point Sarah doesn't deactivate that trance, she may not understand why later in life, wave after wave of that original fear keeps surfacing. Not knowing what else to do, Sarah may turn to any number of distractions—including addictions and denial—so she doesn't have to feel that again.

ENERGY IS DESIGNED TO *MOVE, NOT FREEZE*

Emotions are a form of energy that animate us and add juice and variety to life. Ideally, we can sense an emotion in the body —joy, enthusiasm, confusion, grief—and then express them out of our body and into the world. Watch young kids do this with mastery. When a kid gets mad, they make an angry face, growl, or scream or cry. In other words, they express that energy out of their body. Then the emotion is gone. They've allowed the energy of that emotion to finish its trajectory out of the body. Basic physics tells us that energy by its nature, moves.

It's a relief to know the trauma stuck inside is merely the energy of old emotions that are trying to *finish their trajectory out of the body.*

If the emotional energy doesn't find a way out of the body, it will keep sending signals that we eventually recognize as symptoms. Anxiety. Addiction. Ulcers. IBS. Being accident prone. Depression. Fibromyalgia. Panic attacks. These symptoms that manifest in our lives are frustrating, inconvenient, and often painful, but they are not our enemies. They are often deeply rooted in a survival trance. Think of your symptoms as a clear message from the frozen energies in you, trying to get your attention.

That part of you still in survival trance only wants to feel safe
and have a chance to rest and recover.

YES, I DEACTIVATED MY TRANCE!

I've learned that if your nervous system can activate a trance in you, it can also deactivate it. My 15-year-old self is no longer frozen in trance. I have deactivated that old survival trance and several others I've collected over my lifetime. It's surprisingly simple to do. With the guidance of a BodyMind Bridge practitioner, I journeyed into my deeper mind, found that young teen self and got her out of that basement. While in my deeper mind, I looked into her eyes and asked what she needed. She said, "I just want to feel safe." So, I invited her to come home, to be in the world with me in present time.

Today, she is safe. I've recovered my personal power taken from me so many years ago. I feel a shift in my body, in my heart, and in my mind.

In lieu of having a trained BodyMind Bridge practitioner to work with, you can do similar work using the *Self Rescue Interventions* in Chapters 6 and 7. When you learn to deactivate your own survival trance, you move out of the grip your history has on you. The old memories don't disappear. They just transform into distant black and white photographs that have no more emotional hooks in you.

What emerges is a full sensory understanding of your life, experienced in present time.

The Invite to Write!
When we write, more information bubbles up from our healing mind.

---

1. Was there ever a time when your body shook and trembled after a scare like the young Impala in this chapter? What do you recall from this experience? Write your thoughts here.

2. Have you ever felt frozen from fear? If so, bring to mind an image of that younger self. About how old were you? In your mind's eye, see any details—what you were wearing, where you were located (home, school, backyard etc.)? Describe it here.

3. Close your eyes. Sense if there is a place in your body where you notice a part of you still in a survival trance. One way to do this is to ask, "Where do I hold my fear?" Write about this here.

NOTES

"The genius inside a person wants activity. It's connected to the stars; it's connected to a spark and it wants to burn and it wants to make and it wants to create and it has gifts to give. That is the nature of inner genius."

—Michael Meade

2

WHAT IF YOU KNEW AND TRUSTED YOUR MIND?

"How many mental health problems start as attempts to cope with the unbearable physical pain of our emotions? The solution requires finding ways to alter the inner sensory landscape of our bodies."
—Bessel A. van der Kolk, The Body Keeps the Score

MIND SATURATES YOUR BODY

People in trauma often don't trust their minds, especially their deeper, or subconscious, mind. All the secrets and bottled emotions that are stored there seem to taunt and tantalize. The feeling is that it's a scary place, and that to go there is to lose control. It feels that way, yes. But what if you *were* in control the entire time you looked inside? This changes the game.

Once you are able to do this—to feel safe enough and in control enough to explore and resolve those secrets and emotions, you will discover something extraordinary. Your mind is a field of consciousness that is your ally and knows how you can heal. It has a remedy that is specific to *you*, to your depression or anxiety, to your aches and pains, your addictions, and your sabotaging behaviors. This deeper part of your mind saturates your body and runs all your complex biological systems—respiration, digestion, hormonal releases, blood chemistry, and liver functions. These are all orchestrated by this highly intelligent bodymind. For example, we haven't a clue how to trigger digestion of our meals or how to release our hormones. But the intelligent mind in our body—our bodymind—takes care of that for us.

→→→ ✦ ←←←

Your mind is a field of consciousness that is your ally and knows how you can heal.

→→→ ✦ ←←←

YOUR OUTER AND INNER MIND

There are different regions to your mind. The surface region, or conscious mind, is aware of your outer world, and the deeper levels of mind, or subconscious, are aware of your inner world. Using the example of an iceberg, your conscious mind makes up approximately 10% of your entire waking mind, and the deeper levels make up 90%.

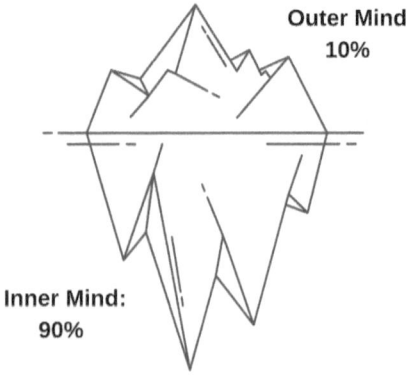

Outer Mind: 10%

Inner Mind: 90%

Even though all the regions are functioning and interacting with one another, this 90% percent is a huge resource for us. It contains our wisdom, our intuition, and our innate connections to the life force. It also holds our traumatized parts until we learn how to rescue them out of the depths. This can be done once your conscious mind steps up and leads this search and rescue mission.

⟶⟩⟩⟩ ✣ ⟨⟨⟨⟵

To deactivate your survival trance, your outer mind must communicate with the inner mind.

⟶⟩⟩⟩ ✣ ⟨⟨⟨⟵

A VERY USEFUL MAP OF YOUR MIND

If you want to trust your mind and feel comfortable in your body, it helps to see a map that shows the levels of your mind and explains the purpose of each. Following is a look at the Map of Your Mind, revealing the four most common brainwaves. If you want more detail, I recommend the more extensive explanation in my book, *BodyMind Bridge and the Self-Healing Mind.*

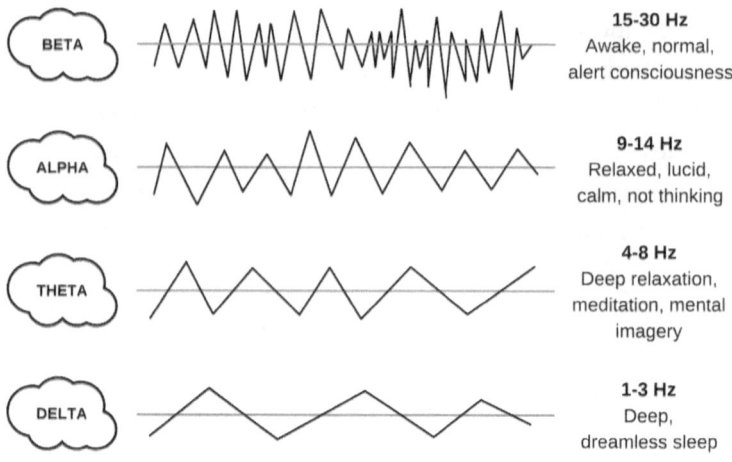

YOUR OUTER WORLD—10% OF YOUR WAKING MIND

The fastest brain wave in this chart is Beta. It has two distinct regions: low-to-mid beta and hyper-beta. One indicates health, and the other, anxiety.

Low-to-mid beta frequencies register on the EEG, or electroencephalograph at 13-20 Hz. When your brain is generating these beta brainwaves, you are connected to the surface mind that is focused on your outer world. Beta mind is also called the conscious mind. Your adult self, your personality, and ego all occupy this beta level of mind. This is also where your reasoning, logic, and basic decision-making abilities are found.

Beta mind must be functioning well if you are to be happy and productive in your life. Its job is to manifest in the outer world the inspiration and guidance that bubbles up from the deeper mind.

NOTE: High Beta Frequencies (20-30 Hz) are faster than beta and develop when we are caught in a loop of fear and anxiety. High beta is the land of worry and dread. Apprehensions are hard to rein in, and you may have trouble trying to focus or sleep. If left unchecked, high beta brain waves can affect both your mental and physical health.

YOUR INNER WORLD: 90% OF YOUR WAKING MIND

Alpha and theta brainwave frequencies are associated with your deeper waking mind.

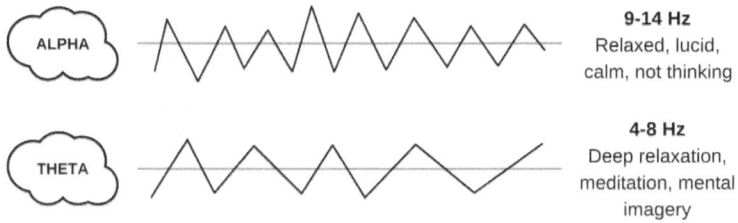

ALPHA

9-14 Hz
Relaxed, lucid,
calm, not thinking

THETA

4-8 Hz
Deep relaxation,
meditation, mental
imagery

Alpha frequencies (9-14 Hz) are slower than beta and associated with relaxation in both body and mind. This is the realm of meditation and contemplative prayer.

If you want to move into your alpha mind, the formula is simple. Close your eyes and observe your breathing. Place full attention on your lungs breathing, and you will move your brain waves into alpha. People have done this for millennia to easily and automatically slow brain waves into the quieter alpha range.

Another way to move into alpha waves is to step outside and notice the natural world. When you fully notice, for example, the chickadee in your apple tree, the clouds in the sky, or hear the patter of rain on the window, your mind easily shifts into alpha. Nature is an alpha wonderland! (This assumes you are not on a device or otherwise distracted by your thinking beta mind.) Alpha happens automatically the moment you move your gaze out the window at the natural world.

→›››‹‹←

This dive into our calmer alpha mind gifts us with precious moments of inner rest, away from our thinking mind and the demands of the outer world.

→›››‹‹←

Theta frequencies (4-8 Hz) are deeper and slower than alpha. Right before you nod off to sleep, when you are in that drifty, groggy state this is what theta feels like. You are still awake in theta, meaning if someone were to walk into the room, you could open your eyes to see who it is.

Theta frequencies also open us to the gift of our innate healing abilities. Your theta mind produces a deep body wisdom that has specific instructions you need to remedy your specific health concerns—whether mental, emotional, or physical.

REVEALED: YOUR TRAUMA IS STORED IN THE ALPHA AND THETA LEVELS OF YOUR MIND!

Here's the rest of the alpha/theta story . . . This is where you can access those younger selves still frozen in survival trance. When in alpha (or the deeper theta level of mind) you give your adult self the grace to meet with them, tend to their wounding, and invite them to come home into present time with you.

Consider this possibility for even a moment, and you'll see the incredible gift it is that the average person can release the survival trance they have been carrying. No pharmaceutical or surgery or therapy can do this for us. This is the healing work we get to participate in!

Delta frequencies (1-3 Hz) are not part of your waking mind, and instead mark the land of deep and dreamless sleep. This is where deep restorative sleep occurs. Cells get the chance to repair, and all thoughts and events of your day are organized and placed in the proper files. When your brain is generating delta waves, you have loss of body awareness and don't even know you exist.

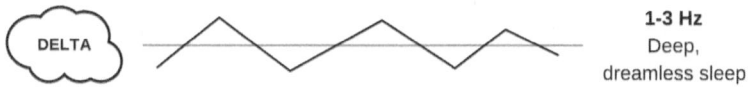

DELTA — 1-3 Hz Deep, dreamless sleep

A Summary of Brainwaves in your Outer and Inner World

1. Outer Mind
a. Beta—the on-task, capable adult, thinking part of your mind
b. Hyper beta—when beta mind becomes trapped in a loop of fear

2. Inner Mind
a. Alpha—the relaxed, quiet mind
b. Theta—holds wisdom and healing information

WHEN WILL YOU BE READY FOR THIS?

You are on your own timeline when it comes to participating in your healing. There is a readiness factor at play here. Some people hit rock bottom before they give a voice to that hurting part of themselves. Do you wonder if you are even capable of doing this inner healing? Or if you'll be safe? Consider these questions, and then take another look at your own readiness.

- What if you are in control during the entire healing experience?
- What if you can gently move into deeper levels of mind, find that younger self still frozen in survival trance, and make decisions for their care?
- What if you can do this inner work and not feel re-traumatized?

This is how I structured the Self-Rescue Interventions in this book —*you* are in control, *you* do the search and rescue of a younger self, and *you* don't get retraumatized, because, well, you choose what you experience. Deep self-healing can happen. When you let your outer mind hear the messages that the inner mind is broadcasting, worlds of possibilities open. The goal of the Self-Rescue Interventions is to *allow beta mind to access the memory so it can resolve it.* All the instructions you need to bridge your outer mind with your inner mind are in Chapters 6 and 7. This inner work can be done with a certified BodyMind Bridge practitioner to guide you, with a caring friend, or on your own. However you choose to do it, the goal is to restore communication between all levels of your waking mind.

AMANDA

Amanda could not stop crying and was baffled by her tears. She had been through breakups before, but it was never like this. This was her first relationship with a woman, and when her girlfriend suddenly ended it, something in Amanda collapsed. Tears soaked her sleeves day and night. She curled up in bed with a box of tissues and called in sick for over a week. Her eyes were red and exhausted.

She went to therapy, and even after several appointments, had no relief. The sobbing continued. Her therapist was stumped and referred her for a BodyMind Bridge session.

"I don't understand," Amanda began. Her long hair was piled on top of her head and flopped over to form a question mark. "It makes no sense why I'm so upset. I knew all along it wouldn't last. So, when she ended it, I thought, oh well, life goes on. But then boom! I was flooded with such grief, and I *cannot* figure out why."

Amanda's outer mind could not find an explanation for her upset. It pawed at thin air, looking for a reason. But her deeper mind knew.

As a young teen, her emotionally distant mother left the family. This devastated the young Amanda so deeply that she cut herself off from remembering how it felt. Her nervous system moved her into a survival trance to help her cope. The survival trance did its job and got her through the hard years and into adulthood, yet it also meant one day she would need to recall and release the suffering her younger self was still feeling, buried deep in her psyche. Her overwhelming tears brought her to her BodyMind Bridge session. She was ready.

Her BodyMind Bridge session

During her session, when she was in her relaxed alpha mind, Amanda imagined resting in a forested area under a blue sky. She smelled the scent of pine and felt the warm sun on her face and neck. When she invited an inner advisor to join her to help her understand her dilemma, the advisor that showed up was not who she expected.

"It's my mom," she said with a set jaw. "I don't want to talk with her."

"Ok," I replied. "This is *your* inner world, and you are in charge here. You can ask her to leave if you want."

"I told her to sit behind some trees on the other side of the field."

After a pause, she reconsidered. "Well, I guess I do want to talk to her."

"Go ahead and do that," I said.

As she had the inner conversation with her mom, her face showed rigid anger, which melted into grief.

Amanda whimpered, "So I just asked mom why she left me ... She answered by showing me all the times she was sick. Mentally, I mean. I guess I forgot about that. I remember now."

She continued, "I was 13 when she left. That day when I got home from school she was gone. Just gone. All her stuff. Everything. And nobody talked about it."

I asked, "And so, do you understand now why she left?"

"Yes, she had to go to a mental hospital."

Amanda gasped. She took a deep breath, and then sobbed —the kind of sobbing that is soul deep and cleansing. I knew that she had just broken through her survival trance.

She squeezed out her words between sobs. "I thought . . . she abandoned me . . . Well, she did, but now I get it. She just told me how sorry she is. I let her hug me."

When Amanda was abandoned as a young teen, part of her could not cope, and her nervous system placed her in a survival trance to cushion her from the grief and confusion. Now that her deeper mind shared the reason for her tears, she understood that her uncontrollable crying was triggered when her girlfriend abandoned her.

For the first time she felt compassion for her mom's struggle with mental illness and was able to forgive her.

NOW, BRIDGE OUTER WITH INNER

Beta can't do it alone. If emotional bombshells take over your mood, your outlook, or endanger your relationships, beta isn't equipped to know what to do. The reasoning and logic of your beta mind comes up short because there is nothing reasonable or logical about how trauma affects us so deeply. Your beta mind is not designed to do the major overhauls you want in your life. Only a unified mind can do this, meaning all levels are hearing one another.

DISTRACTIONS HAVE A PURPOSE, TOO

When your mind is not running on all cylinders, when we aren't hearing the deeper mind, we turn to distractions to get us through. We stay busy. We find solace in food or drugs or shopping. TV blasts in the background to shield us from uninvited voices that come in the quiet. We even create drama for a bit of quick relief, though our soul craves silence and deep rest.

All this effort just so we can avoid the very thing we need—connection to our inner life!

It's taken me years to stop judging my own distractions. I once thought they were a weakness. Now I see them more as benevolent placeholders. They muffled any awareness of the wounds I held inside and gave me the time I needed to do my inner work. Yet all the while I did this self-cocooning, I'd still sense a younger me whispering, "Excuse me, but I'm still in here and I just want to come home. I just want to come out of this trance and into the light of day and be safe—with you."

That little kid was my beacon. She waited patiently until I decided to let myself see her, feel her, and indeed invite her home.

The Invite to Write!
When we write, more information bubbles up from our healing mind.

---

1. When it comes to participating in your healing, you are on your own timeline. On a scale from 1–100, how do you gauge your readiness currently in your life? What do you notice about this number?

2. All three levels of the waking mind—beta, alpha and theta—are meant to collaborate so you can have the optimum life experience. Is your outer mind aware of what your inner mind hears? If not, what occurred to cut you off from this awareness?

3. How does it feel to know you can interact with that younger part of you and deactivate their (your!) survival trance? Exciting? Scary? Freeing? Threatening? Write your thoughts here.

NOTES

*"If the trauma in you seems small and insignificant,
you might look again through more compassionate eyes.
Our stories carry power."*

—the author

3

HOW DID THEY DEACTIVATE THEIR SURVIVAL TRANCES?

"It was me who found the grief in my body and let it go!"
—Emily, a BodyMind Bridge client

The stories in this chapter come from people who have deactivated their survival trances during a BodyMind Bridge session, yet the same outcomes are possible with the Self-Rescue Interventions waiting for you in part two of this book. I selected the client stories in this chapter to make three points:

1. Humans experience a wide variety of traumatic events.
2. It's time to debunk the idea that only hugely terrifying events leave their mark on us.
3. All people carry trauma. It's part of the human experience.

BUT FIRST, WHAT'S YOUR STORY?

Your life story matters. All the good, bad, happy, sad you have felt is the mark of a life fully lived. Even the untold or unexpressed secrets are part of your story. Yet when you speak those secrets out loud, you release any grip they have had on you. Keeping them inside enslaves you. Speak them out loud, and they begin to move out of that storehouse in your inner mind and into the outer world.

Consider your own life story for a moment. What was it like to grow up in *your* house with *your* family in *your* neighborhood? In your lifetime you've cobbled together a unique life story with these as your backdrop. Maybe you were lucky enough to have helpful guidance from an adult or two along the way, or like a lot of kids, you were left to figure things out on your own. This is especially true of kids suffering from trauma.

⌖

It's a challenge to suffer from trauma and live a fully engaged life.

⌖

If the trauma you carry seems insignificant when compared to what others have gone through, you might look again through more compassionate eyes. Even minor traumatic events can pile up over time and cause distress. People tend to minimize the effect their survival trances have on their lives, mostly because they aren't ready to feel them and wouldn't know what to do with them if they did.

Most traumatic experiences hover somewhere between the two extremes. No matter how protected you thought you were growing up, the arc of your life story was likely sprinkled with moments and events that overwhelmed your senses and immediately ushered you into what is meant to be the temporary safety zone of a survival trance. It's a challenge to suffer from trauma *and* live a fully engaged life. Trauma occupies too much precious space in your body and psyche. It conjures up symptoms such as ulcers, migraines, irritable bowels, and high blood pressure. Not because they are an enemy. Quite the opposite. The emotional and physical symptoms we feel in our bodies are doing their job—waving red flags and signaling us that something within needs our attention if we are to heal.

Do the inner work as outlined in this book, and you'll discover how and why you activated your own survival trances—and how to *deactivate* them. It is possible to convert your fear into freedom, anger into calm, shame into worthiness, and abandonment into belonging.

CLIENTS' STORIES

These stories come from regular people who endured their own versions of trauma and who were at the mercy of old emotions. They had never heard of the concept of a survival trance and had no idea they could do something about it. Each was ready to find the frozen places in them and free those captive energies. You too can resolve the survival trances in you. There are younger selves in you who are awaiting your arrival.

Note on Client Privacy: Each of the following stories is a shortened version of the full dialog spoken during BodyMind Bridge sessions. Details are based on my session notes. To honor their inner journey and to safeguard their privacy, I've changed the names and locations of each client.

ETHAN—A TODDLER OSTRACIZED BY FAMILY

Cause of survival trance: deep guilt and shame

Ethan slumped in a soft chair in my office when he began his session with me. His body was draped in sweatpants and a hoodie—both too large for his frame—as though he was trying to disappear. He scratched his gritty chin and exhaled a long sigh. At 27, he described himself saying, "I'm so depressed that I just can't do anything. I've been useless all my life." He came to his BodyMind Bridge session with the hope that maybe he could release some of the guilt and grief that he'd carried around for most of his life.

"Do you recall when the depression started?" I asked.

"Sure, I do." His voice was raspy and quiet, as though his vocal cords hadn't been introduced to the air in his lungs.

"It started when I was a little kid, the morning I walked into the kitchen and saw my baby sister choking in her highchair," he began. "I was just a little 2-year-old kid in saggy diapers." He paused, remembering. He grabbed his sleeve as tears breached his lower lid and fell to his cheek.

"Yep, my sister died . . . I've seen lots of therapists, especially in my teens when all I wanted to do was die. They put me on Prozac and other stuff, which made me worse. I've been on and off meds ever since, and I hate them."

Ethan's backstory

"When I toddled into the kitchen that morning my sister was in her highchair, coughing and choking. I didn't understand what was happening or what to do, but I did know something was wrong, so I should have done something. I just stood and stared.

I froze. Mom was in the backyard hanging laundry. Dad was upstairs. Nobody knew but me. How can a little kid know what to do in a situation like this?"

"The screen door squeaked open. Mom came in with the clothes basket on her hip and saw my sister slumped over and still. She screamed, *"No, No, No!"* She tried to make my sister breathe and yelled for Dad to call the ambulance. He sprinted downstairs and tried to make her breathe, too. That's the moment he turned to me and screamed: "Why didn't you come get us, Ethan? Why didn't you *do* something?" I remember I fell to the floor. My face crumbled. In that singular moment, I felt banished from all that was good, all that was warm and kind. I knew it was my fault. I spiraled into a dark place." He paused, spinning his oversized watch around his wrist. "Is it even possible for a kid that young to be so depressed?"

Ethan squirmed, absently sipping water. "I've moved through my life in a fog, feeling detached from the people and world around me. In high school I did every drug I could find to stay numb. I had zero self-worth. I've been trapped in a hell of repeating memories that flare up out of nowhere. I even tried to off myself three times, and that landed me in a mental hospital when I was 19. After a few more years trying to recover, my therapist helped pull me out of the deep hole I was in." With a shaky voice he said, "I'm thankful I've begun to function again, but the guilt about my sister's death is still deep inside me, still haunting me. That's when I heard about this BodyMind Bridge thing and decided it was time. I'm ready to release the grip it still has on me."

Ethan's BodyMind Bridge experience, as told by Ethan

During the session, Shuna guided me into my deeper mind, and I found my 2-year-old self in the kitchen just like I remembered. But this time every color and smell and sound in that place was amplified. I wasn't afraid to be in that kitchen because I was on a search and rescue mission that I was ready to do. It felt good to be doing *something*. There was my saggy-diaper self leaning against the fridge. The little guy was trembling, so scared.

Shuna asked me, "Does 2-year-old Ethan know that you, his adult self, is there in the kitchen with him?"

"I don't think so."

"Do you want him to know?"

"Yes. He needs some help."

"Go ahead and let him know you are there with him."

I did. He seemed relieved and started to move toward me but stopped. I watched as he slowly turned around, jerky, like a robot. Then a weird thing happened. A small wooden coffin appeared in the kitchen. He crawled inside and closed the lid.

Shuna asked, "What would you like to do?"

"He can't stay in there. He's so scared."

She gently repeated, "What would you, your capable adult self, like to do?"

"I want to get him out of there."

"Go ahead and do that."

I pried the little coffin open and scooped him up. He clung to me, silent at first. I whispered over and over it wasn't his fault—that he is a little boy and little boys don't know what to do when people are choking. His stiff body began to soften and went heavy in my arms. His chest heaved like he was going to hyperventilate. I just held him as he cried. That's when his tears became mine, and I cried with him, feeling deep release in my own body.

After a while, Shuna said, "If you'd like, you can invite him to come be with you. To come into present time, where he can be a happy little boy again, where he can feel safe and seen. Is that something you'd like to do?"

"Yes. He's been through enough. I want him to know he isn't alone anymore."

"OK. Consider where in your physical body you want him to live, a place in your body where you can feel his presence with you. It's important you sense him with you in present time, in your body."

I thought about this, then swept my hand from belly to chest. "In my core. I want him to be here where he can be with me and know I love him."

"Go ahead and invite him to be with you, in your core."

And I did.

After the session

Immediately after my session ended, I started shaking. A strong trembling moved through my body–like it was letting go of emotional pain. Shuna let me know that yes, my body was naturally releasing the old trauma energy. It lasted a while. To me it seemed like I was feeling all my kid energy again. It took a few days to integrate the experience. I had to remind myself that yes, I really did find my frozen kid self, explained it wasn't his fault, and brought him to be with me in present time. Each day I focused on this, I felt the depression lift more. Now it's been a few weeks. I can still feel his presence in me, his energy, and I'd say my depression is at least 80% better. My life is back on track. And I think it's amazing, that regular people like me can do this.

EMILY—GRIEF DIDN'T SHOW UP ON THE MRI

Cause of survival trance: sudden loss

Emily came to her BodyMind Bridge session wearing a grey and white pin-striped blouse that matched her greying shoulder-length hair. She was 46, living alone, and wracked with depression and grief. "I'm ready to do something really different to get my life back. I just wanna feel like me again."

Emily's backstory

"Before I get into my full story, I have to tell you my dog Max was my best friend," she began. She hesitated as a memory materialized behind her eyes. "I wouldn't admit that to many people, but it's true. Every morning at the same time, I'd grab my yellow umbrella and he'd take me for an early walk in the drizzle. He was a gorgeous golden lab. His tail swooshed with every step. Made me so happy."

"On that morning, the sea fog was thick. I remember wiping the mist off my glasses. I stopped to tie my shoe. Water fell in slow motion from my hood. That's when Max stepped off the curb and in front of a big truck." Emily stopped speaking, sensing the scene for the hundredth time. "I still hear it all so clearly. I knew he was gone. I went into shock and my knees folded. The driver jumped out and tried to hold me up, saying how sorry he was, but his words were muffled and far away. I froze. I think I was screaming inside but not out loud."

She blinked tears and slowly looked back at me. "To this day I can't shake the feeling it was my fault."

"Just a day later, I sunk into a depression. My left shoulder began to hurt. A lot. I saw a therapist to ease my depression and a physical therapist to help with my shoulder pain. Even had an MRI and it showed no tissue damage, no reason for it to be hurting like it did. I soon realized the physical therapy wasn't helping much, and neither were all the therapy sessions. I was ready to quit."

"Then a friend told me about BodyMind Bridge, and I knew I was ready for someone to show me how to *help myself* out of the depression and relieve the shoulder pain."

Emily's BodyMind Bridge experience, as told by Emily

During the session, I sat back in a comfy chair with a blanket over my legs and closed my eyes. With Shuna as my guide, I started observing my breathing, dropped my shoulders, and sank into my chair. After a while, I was really relaxed and in a dreamlike place—she explained this was my alpha mind. I was still drowsy but awake.

Shuna asked me to scan my body and find where I felt the depression. That was easy—it was the heaviness in my chest. I could feel a deep grief stored there. Being in my deeper mind was relaxing. As guided, I slowly exhaled and looked with my mind's eye for an image to show up in my chest, where I felt the heaviness. My chest began to tremble as I waited for the image to come to me. I could feel the grief and guilt wanted to get out of my body.

That's when Max showed up! I did not expect this! He jumped around me, his tongue flapping, flashing his happy eyes. I could even hear him and smell his breath! We got to be together again, and it felt very real. I dropped to my knees and ran my hands through his warm fur, hugging on him.

Somehow, he told me, 'I'm OK, Em. I really am. Please stop blaming yourself. I'm really happy.' Hearing this, sobs burst out of me. Shuna handed me tissues. This deep release drained my heart of guilt and grief. Max just sat there calmly until I was done. A few moments later he grabbed his leash. In the movie in my mind, we walked.

Later, when I opened my eyes to the outer world, I felt so light. The weight on my chest was gone, and my shoulder —the one holding the leash that day—stopped throbbing.

After the session:

Looking back at that session, the coolest thing was that with some guidance, it was *me* who found the grief in my body and let it go. I didn't know I could do that. I deactivated the survival trance that lodged in me a year ago and helped me recover from the shock of losing Max.

TRACEY—TRIGGERED BY LIES

Cause of survival trance: fear and neglect

When I met Tracey, she was a pony-tailed young mom with pursed lips and a distant gaze. An old black Harley jacket hung from her shoulders, and what passed as a smile was a tense jawline, cast in defiance. She booked a BodyMind Bridge session because she kept getting "massively triggered" whenever somebody told a bald- faced lie or refused to take responsibility for their actions. She said, "Today if somebody lies to me or to anyone else, I fly into crazy fits of anger, and say and do things I always regret later. Like it controls me, and I want it to stop. So today, I just want to let go of some of the anger and hurt. I want to be more even keel, ya know? My own kids deserve a mom who doesn't fly off the handle."

Tracey's backstory

"What I remember of my kid years is that dad was a drunk and mad all the time. Nobody felt safe when he was around, but I don't think he hit us. I could handle all that pretty good, but then my mom up and left us when I was in first grade. She just walked out, and nobody told me why. She left me and my little sister with him, and even at a young age I knew he lied about everything. The first big lie was "your mum will come back," but she didn't.

"He also lied about food. 'I'll bring some groceries for you girls tonight.' He'd show up with one crumbled paper bag that wasn't even full. I'd unpack it, all excited. Always there was Coke, chips, baloney, a loaf of bread and a box of cereal. I really wanted eggs and bacon like mom used to make, but that didn't happen. When I complained, he said he'd take us to McDonalds. Another lie. Not only did I have to protect my little sister, *but it also became part of my job to* figure out how to feed us. I recall pouring lots of bowls of corn flakes.

"As I grew up, I just got more pissed off. It seemed like every-body was a liar. I'm tired of always being triggered. So here I am, ready to try this BodyMind Bridge thing." She sat tall in her chair and said, "I'm done with this bullshit."

Note: When a child must fend for themself *and* care for a sibling —this is severe neglect—causing trauma. In Tracey's case, she piled one survival trance onto another. It's how she got through the tough times.

Tracey's BodyMind Bridge experience, as told by Tracey

After Shuna helped me get into my quieter mind and get more relaxed, I began to have visual memories, like movies almost, of times when I was a kid. It wasn't emotional, at least not yet. Instead, I was watching from a distance, not involved. It was like my current adult self was there, watching. Then the scene switched, and I saw a time when I was 7 years old, sitting on the sofa in the living room of the house I grew up in. She was barefoot, in her pajamas, listening to mom and dad fight again. Her hands covered her ears. The noise was unbearable. Somehow, I knew that my little sister was upstairs, awake but silent.

Shuna asked, "Does your younger self know that you— her current adult self—is there with her in the living room?"

"I didn't think so."

"Do you want her to know you are there with her?"

"Heck yeah."

Shuna said, "This is your inner world, so anything is possible here. How do you want to get her attention and introduce yourself to her?"

So, I freeze-framed my screaming parents to shut them up so I could get some peace and let my 7-year-old self know I was there with her. She blinked a few times, then looked me right in the eyes. Somehow, she recognized I was there to help her. That's when she flew into my arms. I held her tight for a long while. I whispered that she was safe now, and that's when we both cried an "everything's gonna be alright" kind of cry. It was great to hold her. It was great to feel safe.

I turned to my freeze-framed parents. They figured out who I was—the adult version of their little girl—and stopped fighting. Their faces were blank like they didn't understand what was happening. It was hard to stay so mad at them. They seemed so lost.

Shuna said, "What would you like to do now?

"To get me and my sister out of this house."

"OK. Do you want to invite both your 7-year-old self and your sister to come be with the adult you, in present time?" she asked.

I did want to do that. I asked them, "You wanna get out of here and come live with me?" They nodded yes. I was still in my deeper mind, and with Shuna's guidance, I prepared a place for them in my heart space. I gathered my younger self and my little sister and brought them home. I felt new energy in me when they showed up in my heart. The three of us hung out and played together in present time, in this new safe place. I felt like my 7-year-old brought lightness into my life, and my little sister brought joy like little kids still have. I can still sense them with me today.

After the session:

It's now been over a week, and I feel a lot lighter. I hardly ever get upset when I hear somebody lie. It's like I have a bigger perspective about it all. I think about all those years that me and my sister had been in shock, so lonely and so afraid, and now we aren't. It makes a big difference in my life to have them back. It's like I undid the emotional hook I took on as a kid and freed up a part of myself that was still hurting. So cool we can do that!

JAKE—SAW THE WRECK COMING

Cause of survival trance: auto accident

Jake decided to try a BodyMind Bridge session because a recent car wreck made him too afraid to use the highway. When I met him, he wore a tan Carhart jacket, hands shoved in the pockets. His hair was close shaven to match his nearly invisible beard. As we began, he appeared agitated, picking at his nails, and tapping both legs under the table. "It's been months since my car wreck and my wife is tired of driving me to work. I tried again a couple weeks ago. I drove to the on ramp and couldn't do it. I pulled over, felt lousy about it, and stared for a while at the traffic. So, I used the back roads, adding an hour to my commute."

Jake's backstory

"I was moving with the traffic, jammin' to some great acoustic tunes, when traffic just stopped. I panicked, glanced in the rear-view mirror and saw a white truck was just about to hit me. I covered my head and held my breath. I went stone cold rigid. What else could I do? The impact snapped my head forward and then slammed me back into the seat several times. I lost consciousness."

Jake woke in the ambulance. His neck was in a heavy brace. "I was strapped down, confused, and fought to get free. I blacked out again."

After weeks of physical therapy for his injured neck, the docs gave him a clean bill of health.

"But my neck still hurt, I started to get bad headaches, and was petrified of getting on the highway. I learned from a coworker there was a way I could deactivate the trauma, and I thought what the heck, I'll give it a try."

Jake's BodyMind Bridge experience, as told by Jake

Once in my quiet mind, I chose to return to that day in the car. I couldn't believe all the details coming up. I could hear the traffic report on the radio and feel the seatbelt tight across my chest. I could even recall what I was thinking right before the accident. It's like I was watching that guy who was me, about to get rear ended.

He looked up at the rear-view mirror and saw the truck about to hit. I started to feel fear bubble up. Shuna said something like, "This is your inner world, Jake, and you can change anything that happened if you want to. What do you want to do?"

So, I decided to stay present and protect him. A ferocity filled my chest and I began to breath deep. Like a Marvel hero, I held my hand up to the truck in the mirror and screamed, "*STOP!*" I kept commanding a new outcome. "*Stop!*" I was saying this out loud.

The truck stopped. I heard no crash. The airbag stayed tucked in the steering wheel. My neck was unscathed. I sat in silence. The next part is hard to describe, but it was so real. A kind of rewind started to unravel the fear I had been holding onto. My breathing slowed. Heart rate returned to normal. I felt my body go limp, and I rested.

A few moments later, my body let the rest of it go. I shook and cried and trembled. All the fear and paralysis stored in me just poured out for several minutes. Then, I was calm to my core.

After the session

A couple days later, I felt clear and relaxed enough to try the highway again. At first, I hesitated. Then that fierceness in my chest showed up. Somehow, I felt safe and knew I was going to be OK. I merged the car into light traffic and exhaled.

MORE EXAMPLES—BUT JUST THE HIGHLIGHTS

Here is a summary of other clients' stories to further illustrate the healing ability embedded in us.

CHRONIC BACK PAIN

Jodi had to stop training for the half marathon in her town. It was painful to even bend over to work in her garden. For years, she had a string of seemingly unrelated injuries keep her from doing the things she loved. She had a hunch something deeper was behind all the pain but didn't know what. Something was keeping her from healing.

During her session she blurted, "What's holding me down?"

A scene opened in her mind's eye. Dad and grandpa were holding her infant-self down in her bassinet, tickling her. They were laughing, thinking it was cute, but her infant-self was wide eyed with fear. Her small body felt overpowered, and she was unable to make a sound.

Her current adult-self stepped in and sent the men away, then looked in the eyes of her infant-self, talked with her and cared for her. Her child-self eventually began to cry, released from the fear. The adult-Jodi then invited her infant-self to come be with her, away from that place, and safe.

A few weeks later, Jodi's back pain lifted, and she felt a freedom to move forward with the things she enjoyed doing.

FEAR OF ABANDONMENT

David's parents divorced when he was 7. Each Saturday, he would sit on the front porch with his suitcase packed, waiting for dad to pick him up. Week after week, dad didn't show. No phone call. No explanation. Just a promise he'd be there the next time. This is when David began to blame himself for not being lovable enough or important enough for dad to spend time with him. In his young heart and soul, he felt abandoned and unworthy.

During his session, adult Dave found his younger self on those steps. He sat next to little David, introduced himself, and then listened to him sob out his hurt. Little David nestled in his arms and quieted, feeling seen and important. Adult Dave bundled him up, grabbed his suitcase, and brought him into present time to be with his adult self, safe and loved.

PROTECTED BY FOOD

Courtney endured sexual abuse from age 6 to 13. Under direct threat from the abuser, she told no one. Each time it happened she just slipped out of her body and traveled to an elaborate place of refuge forged in her imagination. This was her survival trance. To keep the memories away, she soon found the comfort she needed in food. As she gained weight, she hated herself, then ate more. She began Cognitive Behavioral Therapy and continued this for several years. She was given anxiety meds.

Now 34 years old, Courtney came to her BodyMind Bridge session because she wanted a new relationship with food. Like the others in the stories above, she located her younger self, protected her from the abuser, and invited her home. In this case, once Courtney was able to release the heaviness felt by her abused younger self, she began to safely release the extra weight. With further help from a wellness coach, she learned to use food to nourish instead of harm.

IDIOPATHIC HIP PAIN

Lori's hip pain began when she left her marriage, and the orthopedic doctor could not find any physical cause. For eleven years her ex-husband had kept her on a short leash, close to home. She was afraid all the time, yet with support from friends and family, eventually found the courage to leave.

During Lori's BodyMind Bridge session, she moved her deep awareness directly to the pain in her hip. The image that surfaced was her ex-husband's face. She asked, "Why are you here?"

He answered, "If you won't be with me then I don't want you to move on with your life."

She found her voice and boldly spoke her truth to him, telling him she was a sovereign being and he had no place in her life. The image of him vanished. Three days later Lori's hip pain stopped.

The Invite to Write!
When we write, more information bubbles up from our healing mind.

---

1. Consider your own life story for a moment. How was your emotional self shaped as you grew up in your house with *your* family in *your* neighborhood?

2. Have you ever compared your survival trance to someone else's and then downplayed or minimized the effect it had on you?

3. Which of the stories in this chapter had the most impact on you? Which felt the closest to your own story?

NOTES

PART TWO:

THREE TIME-DEPENDENT REMEDIES

"The best time to purge the adrenaline from your system is immediately after the experience. Let your body shake."

—*the author*

4

IMMEDIATELY AFTER THE INCIDENT HAPPENS— DISCHARGE THAT ADRENALINE!

*"Shaking can stop the damaging effects
that a recent frightening event can cause."*
—the author

SHAKE RATTLE AND ROLL

As soon as possible after a traumatic incident, it is essential to discharge the fight or flight chemicals out of your body. This will reset your nervous system and slowly return you to a metabolic equilibrium.

You do this by literally shaking the adrenaline and fear-based chemicals out of your body with as much gusto as you can, but only if you are safe and physically unhurt. This will allow the trauma to exit your body and prevent the fear from lodging in your psyche. Shaking is one of four things you can do to stop the damaging effects—physical and emotional—that a recent frightening event can cause. All four steps are below.

But first, check these two things:

1. Is the danger gone, and are you safe?

2. Are you physically unharmed?

If the answer is *YES* to both, do these four things:

1. Shake. Tremble.

Turn your attention to sensations in your body and notice that it wants to tremble and shake, and then let it. We often feel this begin in our core and spread to our limbs. If you haven't yet noticed your body's natural, involuntary shaking response, then *you* can get the adrenaline release started by choosing to shake your arms and legs. Exaggerate those movements until the body takes over and begins its own instinctive shaking.

2. Yell. Scream.

Breathe forcefully in and out and let any sound out. This helps the survival energy to move out of the body.

3. If there are tears, let them fly.

4. Do this until you are spent.

When your body is done shaking and the last bit of sound is squeaked from your lungs, congratulations! You have prevented the fear from lodging in your deeper mind, and you won't have to deal with a survival trance. You will feel spent and calm. This is a huge relief.

If people see you shaking and yelling and they seem alarmed, tell them you are OK. Tell them you are letting go of the trauma so it doesn't stay in you. If need be, find a private place to release the adrenaline and survival energy out of your system.

DON'T WAIT

The best time to purge the adrenaline from your system is immediately after the experience. If you must wait, do this as soon as possible. Your shaking and trembling and tears and yelling all move the pent-up survival energy out of your body and release any emotional harm that you took on during the incident.

Immediately following the incident, your intelligent body automatically begins to remove that disruptive energy and excess adrenaline out of the body. It begins to tremble, then if we let it, the trembling amps into shaking. This simple action erases the after-effects of trauma.

There is a section in Chapter 1: *If You Can't Run or Fight, You Freeze* that you might read again. It will help you recall the significance of shaking and trembling and how it improves your wellbeing when done soon after the trauma.

Teach your kids and grandkids that the trembling is a good thing and to let their bodies and nervous systems do their thing. Nobody has to suffer from the effects of a frightening incident in their life. All they need to do is shake it out!

Animals instinctively tremble and shake to rid their systems of the fight/flight chemicals in their body. In the following story, if Beth had known to do the same, she could have erased the traumatic energy from her own body and psyche.

BETH AND SALSA

Beth in California was walking her new dog, Salsa, when a neighbor's bigger dog jumped out of the bushes and lunged for her pup, teeth snapping. Beth was terrified and immediately froze in shock. Salsa's frantic yelps snapped her out of her shock, and she grunted to pull the dogs apart.

As Beth tells it, "A second later, the guy who owns the dog came crashing down the driveway, and I couldn't believe it—*he yelled at me*! His face was vicious. I froze again—this time terrified of him. He pulled his dog back, and I just stood there in a daze, hugging my whimpering pup."

A quick inspection showed that Salsa had a few scrapes, but nothing life threatening. Physically, both dog and human were unhurt. However, both experienced a sudden threatening attack and the helplessness of overwhelm. The attack that lasted only a minute, looked like this: unexpected danger shocked them, adrenaline was dumped into their bloodstreams, they couldn't fight or run, so both dog and human dissociated and went into a survival trance.

In her arms, Beth felt her dog begin to tremble, then violently shake. "I held him tighter, trying to calm him down but he just shook more and more. Much later I learned that if I had done the same thing, I would have felt much better."

The key to diverting the effects of traumatic events is to discharge the adrenaline out of the body as soon as possible, and little Salsa demonstrated this for Beth.

FRANK AND HIS CAFÉ

Frank lived in downtown San Francisco and dreamed of owning his own café, where neighbors and office workers could gather for yummy pastries and a good cup of coffee.

He found a vacant building in the perfect location close to his apartment. He negotiated the lease, secured a business loan, and then spent months artfully remodeling and upgrading the decor. On opening day, he greeted a line of eager customers at the door. Soon, Frank's café was buzzing with constant activity. It was warm, welcoming, and an instant hit. He was so happy.

A year later, his beloved café was gone. "I was walking to work one chilly morning and heard firetrucks up the street. I turned the corner and my feet stopped. It was surreal. I saw my café on fire. The heat shattered windows and blew shards of glass across the street. People screamed and ran for safety. I froze, not believing. I could even feel myself drifting away.

"Then I remembered I read how to snap out of this type of trance I was going in. So, I dropped to my knees, and I wailed. I flung my arms to the sky and yelled "Aaagh!" from deep in my belly. I stood, shook my arms, kicked the air, clenched my fists, and let my body shake until it was done. People watched, but didn't intervene. A few minutes later, I slowly stood, somehow calm, and walked over to the firefighters. My head was clear, and I knew I could rebuild. The shock and grief at losing my café would hurt for a while, but I also knew I was over the trauma of it."

If you are in a car accident and not hurt, shake.
If you witness violence and are not hurt, shake.
If you run from a bully and are not hurt, shake.
If your dog is attacked or your café goes up in flames, shake.

To learn more about the physiology of trauma, I recommend any books or YouTube videos by Peter A. Levine, Ph.D.

- *In an Unspoken Voice: How the Body Releases Trauma and Restores Goodness*
- *Waking the Tiger: Healing Trauma*
- *Trauma and Memory: Brain and Body in a Search for the Living Past, A Practical Guide for Understanding and Working with Traumatic Memory*
- *Healing Trauma: Restoring the Wisdom of Your Body*

If the emotional effects of trauma interest you, I recommend

- *Trances People Live*, by Stephen Wolinsky, Ph.D.
- *The Body Keeps the Score*, by Bessel van der Kolk
- *No Bad Parts: Healing Trauma and Restoring Wholeness with the Internal Family Systems Model*, by Richard Schwartz Ph.D. and Alanis Morissette

For a body-centered approach to healing trauma:

- BodyMind Bridge Institute: shunamorelli.com
- Somatic Experiencing®: traumahealing.org

The Invite to Write!
When we write, more information bubbles up from our healing mind.

---

1. If you ever become traumatized from witnessing or experiencing violence, what can you do to help your body automatically dump the adrenaline from your system?

2. In some cultures, public wailing and full-body grieving are encouraged after a traumatic event. What has your culture/upbringing taught you about this?

3. Are there people in your life who would benefit from knowing this simple way to keep trauma from settling in the body? Write their names here.

NOTES

*"No matter how deeply we have been wounded,
when we listen to the inner voice that calls us back to our bodies,
back to wholeness, we begin our journey."*

— Tara Brach

HOW TO PREPARE FOR THE SELF-RESCUE INTERVENTIONS IN CHAPTERS 6 AND 7

"When we have the courage to walk into our story and own it,
we get to write the ending."
—Brene Brown

The most direct and efficient way to work with and release years-old trauma is to go where it is located—in the alpha and theta levels of your mind just below your conscious mind. The survival energies that you didn't release back then are stored in the body until you intervene and give them permission to finish their trajectory out of the body's tissues.

When you move into your deeper mind to do your inner work, you are very much awake and making decisions in your inner world. This is what makes your work so transformative.

WHAT IS A SELF-RESCUE INTERVENTION?

A Self-Rescue Intervention (SRI) is a type of guided visualization that is written so *you can do this inner work yourself.* The words in each SRI gently guide you into your quiet mind where you find a deep body intelligence that will show you how to remedy your own specific trauma—even if it happened years ago. The alpha and theta levels of your mind are ready to share useful information that your conscious mind doesn't have access to on its own.

GENERAL INSTRUCTIONS

STEP 1—FORM YOUR INTENT

Your intent will guide the direction of your inner work. Give yourself the time to write your intent, based on the following three questions.

Answer these questions to get started on your intent:

- What do you want to be different in your life?
- What do you want to shift inside you?
- What is your optimum outcome for doing this inner work?

Tip: An intent is most powerful when you hone it down to a sentence or two, and the words are written in present tense. For example: I am loved vs. I *will be* loved. Notice how differently these two intents feel.

STEP 2—DECIDE TO COLLABORATE OR TO DO THIS SOLO

Collaborate: working with a supportive friend

This work is most effective when another person is there with you—someone who will simply listen to your story and not judge, not try to fix you or cheer you up. Call on a trusted friend, or if you have a therapist, they may want to do this deeper work with you. I've written a book especially for therapists who haven't had this type of training, and it shows them how to easily assist you. The book is *BodyMind Bridge Skills for Therapists*. If you choose to work with another person, give them a printed copy of the SRI you will be using. Their job is to be at your side while they read the SRI to you. Specific instructions are below.

Doing this solo

If you want to do this inner work on your own, there is a way. Simply record the SRI in your own voice or ask a friend to record it in their voice. Be sure to read slowly and include pauses. This is because as we move into our deeper mind, we need more time. Then grab headphones, toss a blanket over yourself, and listen as you follow the prompts at your own pace. Settle in and guide yourself on this healing mission.

Instructions for the supportive friend: You don't have to be any kind of expert here, only a good friend. All you are asked to do is quietly read the self-rescue intervention to them. The words will guide your friend to find their own way to deactivate their survival trance. Below are some instructions to help you to prepare.

. . .

Instructions:

1. Please read the SRI to yourself before you read it aloud for your friend. Become familiar with the content, the wording, and the indicated pauses.
2. Each time you see the ellipsis (. . .) it means to pause for about 10 seconds. This gives your friend the time they need to do the inner work you have just asked them to do.
3. When you are ready to read the SRI to your friend, settle in with a few calm breaths, and speak slowly, with a voice that is quiet and caring.

STEP 3—SPEAK YOUR STORY OUT LOUD

Choose a quiet place where you won't be interrupted and sit with your friend. Ask them to simply hear your story. Tell them it is not their job to try to fix you or to cheer you up or to give any advice. All you need is for them to be with you and to listen deeply to your experience.

Begin by sharing :

- what the incident was like for you
- what you recall, and
- how it still affects you today.

Mention any symptoms that have shown up since the incident. This step is significant, since clearly naming your symptom(s) will aid you in this inner healing journey. Your symptoms could be emotional such as depression, anxiety, or a sense of dread, or you may have a long list of physical symptoms. You may notice *both* emotional and physical symptoms have developed. They tend to be interconnected. For example, ongoing fear can cause digestive difficulties, and grief can trigger headaches and joint pain.

If you are working solo, you could write your story, or say it out loud to your dog or cat. They tend to listen well! The point is that you bring the story out of your body via the spoken word or written on paper.

While you are sharing the details about your trauma, emotions may surface, and this is a good thing. Recall that emotion is a form of energy that is supposed to move. If it has been stuck in your body, the fact that it is surfacing is like striking gold. All emotions are welcome. Have tissue within reach.

STEP 4—WORK WITH THE SELF RESCUE
INTERVENTION

Ask your friend to begin reading the Self-Rescue Intervention. Choose the SRI in Chapter 6 if your incident happened weeks or months ago, and the SRI in Chapter 7 if it's been years to decades. I wrote each specifically for those time frames.

If you are doing this solo, just settle in and listen to the recording of the SRI you have made.

Whether with a friend or on your own, you will search for the younger part of you who still holds the fear, and then rescue them from the frozen state they are in. No worries about how to do all this—it is written in the Self-Rescue Intervention you have chosen.

The Invite to Write!

When we write, more information bubbles up from our healing mind.

---

1. Your intent is crafted with your full waking mind, meaning beta mind collaborated with your alpha/theta wisdom. How has your intent guided you to deactivate your survival trances? Write your intent here.

2. Will you to choose to work with another person on your Self-Rescue Intervention, or do this solo? What thoughts led to your decision?

3. When you share your story with others, are there any important details you leave out? If so, write them here. Naming the hidden details help with the healing process.

NOTES

"The emotion swirling in you is not an enemy.
It is on your side and just wants out of the body.
It wants you to be well."

—*the author*

6

YOUR SELF-RESCUE
INTERVENTION FOR WEEKS TO
MONTHS AFTER THE INCIDENT

"The privilege of a lifetime is to become who you truly are."
—*Carl Jung*

In Chapter 4, I described how to restore your equilibrium and reset your nervous system by shaking the adrenaline and fear out of your body as soon as possible after a traumatic incident. If you couldn't do this when it happened, it's OK. Even if it happened weeks or months ago, you can still work directly with the part of you who lived through it and is still experiencing the trauma.

To do this you have to go where the trauma is located. It isn't floating unmoored in the cosmos—it is anchored in your body. The emotions linked to your survival trances are stored in your organs and tissues. In other words, your hurting self can be found in the quiet, alpha/theta levels of mind that saturate your *body*. You can find that frozen part of you when you enter this deep healing mind—your bodymind. This is surprisingly easy to do. The remedy I offer in this chapter will be your guide.

—→⟫ ✦ ⟪←—

You must go where the trauma is located.
It isn't floating unmoored in the cosmos.
It is anchored in your body.

—→⟫ ✦ ⟪←—

IT'S IN THE BODY

Trauma is made tangible in the body. Whenever we have an incomplete experience, meaning we can't get the fear out at the time of the trauma, it gets stored in the energetic systems of our body and we feel it in our body. For example, heaviness in your chest, churning in your gut, or throbbing in your head are symptoms that are often linked to a traumatic incident. The primary intelligence that saturates your physical body is hoping that one day you'll find how to resolve the trance and get your life back.

Since most of us don't know how to do this, we endure it, smile weakly, and proclaim we are OK. We continue to get triggered and feel like we're at the mercy of the dread in us. But it's helpful to know this unrest has another purpose. Think of it as a messenger, a wisdom in you, prompting you to deactivate the emotional hook, the trance caused by the trauma.

The flashbacks and fast-beating heart are there to remind you that your mission is to find a way to release the trauma. There are many new therapies and methods that can guide you to do this. Somatic Experiencing®, Holotropic Breathwork®, ketamine and psilocybin therapies, EMDR (Eye Movement Desensitization and Reprocessing) and the BodyMind Bridge™ System of Self-Healing are all available for this purpose.

⟿ ✣ ⟿

The unrest in you is a messenger, a wisdom in the body prompting you to deactivate the emotional hook caused by the trauma.

⟿ ✣ ⟿

NO MORE BAND AIDS

Talking about our trauma helps us cope in the short term, but it doesn't get to the root cause. We can talk forever, and nothing changes. All the angst we report to anyone who will listen is done with our surface mind, the beta level. It is our attempt to take some of the inner pressure off, but it's temporary.

Another way to cope is to keep it to ourselves and not tell a soul, hoping it will fade over time. Either way, we remain stuck in the surface level of our minds, amping it into the anxiety-filled hyper beta range and increasing our misery.

To make lasting change, we can choose to gently remove the Band-Aid and care for the wound inside. This is where the Self-Rescue Intervention comes in. This is a tool that cares for the wound.

WHAT IS A SELF-RESCUE INTERVENTION?

A Self-Rescue Intervention (SRI) provides a framework for you to do a search and rescue with the younger self who is still hunkered down in survival trance. Think of an SRI as a written guide, using carefully chosen words to lead you on your inner mission. It is similar to a guided visualization—with one big difference: The Self-Rescue Intervention is designed for *you* to be in charge of your own inner work. *You* interact with that younger part of yourself while in your relaxed deeper mind. *You* make all the decisions to help them out of the survival trance and invite them to come safely home and into the present time.

I have written and used these SRIs with hundreds of clients, enabling them to deactivate their survival trance and ease the impact of their trauma. The impressive thing is *they* did this inner work, made all the decisions while in their deeper mind, and created the results they intended—to find and rescue the part of them still suffering from the survival trance.

SAFETY—THE GOLDEN TICKET

Right now, in this moment, you are safe. The incident happened, it is over, and now you are safe. But the parts of you in survival trance don't know that. They are still in shock, still in your body, and still afraid. *They need your permission to come home, and be safe, with you, today.* This is the golden ticket that will prevent a survival trance from taking root.

Please Note: Before you use the Self-Rescue Intervention below, read the important instructions in Chapter 5. There you will learn how to choose and instruct the person who will assist you and be at your side.

SELF-RESCUE INTERVENTION FOR WEEKS TO MONTHS AFTER THE INCIDENT

Prep: Find a comfortable position. Cover yourself with a blanket or have one nearby. If you are working with a friend, they will read this Self-Rescue Intervention to you as instructed in

Chapter 5. If you are working on your own, record this SRI in your own voice. Then grab headphones and settle in.

The SRI:

When you are ready, slowly and gently close your eyes . . . And now, move your awareness to your lungs, and find your breath . . . Begin to notice the rhythm of your breathing . . . Notice the rise and fall of your chest . . . There is no need to change the way you are breathing. Simply observe your breath . . . If you'd like you can drop your shoulders . . . Relax your jaw . . .

Continue to observe your breath, and allow yourself to move more deeply into your relaxed body, relaxed mind.

And now, slowly move your awareness to your physical body . . . Take a moment and scan your body . . . Notice a place in your body where you sense any distress left by the trauma. In other words, locate a place in your body where you sense the trauma is being held for you. (Pause for 20 seconds) If you'd like, you can place a hand there. And now, just notice the sensation in your body . . .

And now, begin to sense the part of you who experienced the incident, the younger one still suffering from the trauma. You might see them clearly, or just have a strong sense of their presence . . .

When you sense that your younger self has arrived, take a moment, and notice any details about them. For example, notice what they are wearing . . .

And now, notice where they are. Sense any details of

their surroundings . . .

If you'd like, let your younger self know that you are there to help them release the trauma and get them to safety . . . Take a moment and notice if you able to see their eyes . . . If possible, gently make eye contact with them . . .

And now, ask what they need . . . Listen to them deeply. (Pause for 45 seconds)

. . . Since this is *your* inner world, know it is possible to step in, and *change* any of the details that led to the trauma . . . If you'd like, you can help them change the outcome of their experience.

And now, ask your younger self if they want to shift the outcome of the incident, with your help. Ask if they want to recreate the details that lead to the incident . . . If they want to do this with you, go ahead and re-create the experience. Change it in any way you'd like . . .

Continue to reimagine new details of that day and allow the trauma in your body to find its way out . . . (Pause for 1 minute.)

And now, take a moment and invite your younger self to come home, to be with you in present time . . . Invite them to return with you to the outer world, where they will be safe and seen . . .

If you'd like, choose a place in your body where they can join you once again, a place in your body where they can feel anchored back in the present moment and secure . . .

And now, take a moment and notice the sensations in your body. You may begin to sense trembling or vibration in your core. This is normal. This is your body releasing the pent-up emotional energy from the trauma. Give yourself permission to let your body release . . . It knows how . . . (Pause at least 1 minute)

And now, prepare to return your awareness to the outer world . . . Take a moment and thank your younger self . . . Welcome them *home*.

Take a deep cleansing breath . . . begin to wiggle your fingers and toes . . . stretch if your body wants to stretch, and when you are ready, slowly open your eyes.

Afterward:

Give yourself time to integrate the shift you just made in your inner world. You may feel tired or want to dance. Maybe you want to journal, or step outside and be in nature. Some people are inspired to grab their paints and make art.

Acknowledge that you have just journeyed, wide-eyed, into your helpful deeper mind, received new information, and rescued the part of you that once was hidden and hurting. Now that you have done this inner work, you have increased the amount of energy running through your body!

Be sure to read Chapter 8 so you know what to expect after working with your SRI.

The Invite to Write!
When we write, more information bubbles up from our healing mind.

---

1. When you read in this chapter that your trauma "isn't floating unmoored in the cosmos—it is anchored in your body," did you notice this to be true for you? Where in your body is your trauma tangible?

2. Have you suspected some of your physical or emotional symptoms may be related to your trauma? If so, write about that here.

3. Regarding feeling safe in the world . . . Does something inside you still feel danger, even though you are now safe? Write about this conflict here.

NOTES

"Your memory of an event is not the event itself.
It will hold on to your difficult emotions until you participate
in their emancipation."

—the author

7

YOUR SELF-RESCUE INTERVENTION FOR YEARS/DECADES AFTER THE INCIDENT

"You are not the voice of the mind—you are the one who hears it."
—Michael A. Singer

YOUR SECRET DANCE PARTNER

If years or decades have passed since you experienced the traumatic event, and you weren't able to run or fight, part of you is still stuck in fear. Or anger. Or any number of emotions. Meantime, the years have passed, you've moved on, and ignored the lingering effects of the trauma the best you could. But all this time you have been dancing with that trauma. Back and forth. Dosey-doe. One moment you have your act together, the next moment the trauma barges in and hogs the dance floor. This dance partner is the younger part of you, trying to help you heal.

Don't assume the fear you feel today is in the past. It isn't. Instead, it is in the present time, in you. Yes, the event did happen. Yes, it is part of your *history, but* it is not in the past. The emotional hook attached to it exists in the present time. You feel it in your body. That's why each time the memory pops up and disrupts your life, your face flushes and heart rate triples. But this is good news. It means the part of you who needs your help is *right there*, right in front of you, and easily accessible.

Thankfully, you don't have to relive trauma from your childhood. The reason? That trauma is *still* in your body today, still influencing your life as an adult.

Heres' the distinction:
Yes, it happened in your history, but it is not in the past.
This event from your history is still in present time,
and still happening in you!

NO FUTURE OR PAST

From birth to about 7 years old, your mind functions only in the present time. You have no sense of past or future. (Just say to a 4-year-old, "Get ready honey, we're leaving in 10 minutes," and see how that goes!) Here's the point—when you are in your deeper alpha/theta level of mind, it's the same. There is no sense of a flow of linear time, no past or future—only the present, only now. *This explains why the fears you experienced back then are still present in your awareness today. They are not located in the "past."*

For example, imagine you are a little kid, and a huge dog runs up to you, growls viciously and snaps its teeth—and you freeze. Now you are an adult, and you still feel panic when a big dog crosses your path. Why? The fear still exists in the *present*, not in the past.

YOUR DISTRACTIONS SERVE A PURPOSE, TOO

How many times has a concerned friend or family member said to you, "Just let it go. It happened a long time ago." Or, "Don't let it bother you anymore. There's nothing you can do about it now." They may mean well, but they don't understand that the emotion tied to your trauma is still in you, popping up from your deeper mind, trying to get your attention.

Maybe you think you've dealt with your trauma via years of therapy, or you've used all your favorite distractions to get you through. Talk therapy can certainly help you understand and cope with the trauma, and your distractions provide a buffer for a while. But that hurting younger part of yourself will continue doing all kinds of things to get your attention. You may wonder, "Why do they persist?"

- They want to heal.
- *They need you to participate.*

PARTICIPATION OF YOUR ADULT SELF IS REQUIRED

Before you do this inner work, pause and acknowledge the part of you who is a capable adult—the one who takes care of the daily tasks like getting the kids to school, paying bills, and buying groceries. These types of activities show that you relate with and function well in the outer world. When a person is in touch with reality, they are capable of doing profound inner healing.

I bring this up because some people are so deeply frozen in their trauma, they struggle to even blink and breathe. Daily tasks require a huge effort. Doing the simplest things feels like slogging through wet concrete. If this describes you, hire a therapist to help bolster the capable adult in you. One must nurture a healthy ego-self to do this inner work.

—→》》 ✣ 《《←—

One must nurture a healthy ego-self to do this inner work.
If you can navigate the tasks of day-to-day living,
you can do this deeper work.

—→》》 ✣ 《《←—

YOUR SEARCH AND RESCUE MISSION

We humans are equipped with a nervous system that knows how to survive traumas by harboring them in the alpha/theta portion of the mind. This strategy gets us to adulthood. To go full circle and produce a happy and thriving adult who is free from trauma, one more step remains. *We must return for our younger selves, provide the safety and compassion they need, and invite them to come out of the shadows and into the outer world, to come home.*

If you wonder how to do this, the Self Rescue Intervention (SRI) in this chapter will guide you.

WHAT IS A SELF-RESCUE INTERVENTION?

Note: If you have read Chapter 6, the following description of the SRI will be familiar. I have reiterated it here for readers who jump right to this chapter if their trauma happened years to decades ago.

A Self-Rescue Intervention (SRI) provides a framework to do a search and rescue with the younger self who is still hunkered down in survival trance. Think of an SRI as a written guide, using carefully chosen words to lead you on your inner mission.

It is similar to a guided visualization, with one big difference: The Self-Rescue Intervention is designed to guide *you* to be in charge of your own inner work. *You* interact with that younger part of yourself while in your relaxed deeper mind. *You* make all the decisions to help them out of the survival trance and invite them to come safely home and into the present time.

I have written and used these SRIs with hundreds of clients, enabling them to deactivate their survival trance and ease the impact of their trauma. The impressive thing is *they* did this inner work, made all the decisions while in their deeper mind, and created the results they intended—to find and rescue the part of them still suffering from the survival trance.

PREVENT A SURVIVAL TRANCE FROM TAKING ROOT

Right now, in this moment, you are safe. Yes, the incident happened. And now, logic tells you all is well and you are safe. But the parts of you in survival trance don't know that. They are still in shock, still in your body, and still afraid. *They need your permission to come home, and be safe, with you, today.* This is the golden ticket that will prevent a survival trance from taking root.

Before you work with the Self-Rescue Intervention below, read the important instructions in Chapter 5. There you will learn how to choose and instruct the person who will assist you in this inner work and be at your side.

SELF-RESCUE INTERVENTION FOR YEARS TO DECADES AFTER THE INCIDENT

Prep: Find a comfortable position. Cover yourself with a blanket or have one nearby. If you are working with a friend, they will read the Self-Rescue Intervention to you as instructed in

Chapter 5. If you are working on your own, record this SRI in your own voice. Then, grab headphones and settle in. Have your finger near the pause button to give yourself any extra time you may need.

The SRI:

When you are ready, slowly and gently close your eyes . . . Begin by taking a comfortable breath . . . and as you exhale, slowly move your awareness into your body, into your chest, and find your breath . . . Notice your lungs as they do their fine work . . . Just become aware of your lungs, and begin to observe the rhythm of your breathing . . . You might notice your chest rise and fall as you breathe . . . There is no need to change the way you are breathing. Just observe your breath, as you move your awareness into your body, into your deeper mind . . .

If you'd like, you can lower your shoulders . . . Perhaps relax the muscles in your jaw . . . And now, become aware of the tiny muscles behind your eyes . . . Notice any tension in these tiny muscles behind your eyes, and let that tension go . . . Let your eyes rest.

And now, allow your entire body to surrender to gravity. Just let gravity absorb any remaining tension in your body . . .

And now, to assist you to move yourself a little deeper into your alpha level of mind, imagine you are standing on a path . . . You don't need to see it clearly like a photograph, instead you may simply sense the presence of your path . . . Take a moment and notice what your path is made of . . . your path can be made of anything, such as sand, or moss or green grass . . . And now, in your mind's eye, imagine gazing down at the ground and notice your own feet on this path . . . Focus on the details of your feet. Perhaps your feet are bare, or wearing sandals, or shoes. Just sense any details about your feet as you stand on this path, touching the earth . . . Sense your feet in contact with your path.

And now, I will count backward from 5 to 1. With each number you hear, imagine taking a step down your path, and as you do, allow yourself to move more deeply into your relaxed mind, relaxed body.

Beginning with *5* . . . Take a step down your path, feeling more and more relaxed . . . *4*, Another step down you path, deeper and deeper. Next . . . *3*, Allowing yourself to move more deeply into your quiet healing mind . . . *2*, More and more relaxed . . . And in a moment, when you hear the number 1, you will begin to notice your Inner Sanctuary . . .

Your Inner Sanctuary can be a place in nature, or any place that emerges in your awareness . . . Your inner sanctuary is a place where you are safe, and where you can be fully who you are . . . And **ONE**. And now, sit back and let your Inner Sanctuary come to you, let it emerge in your awareness. (Pause for at least 10 seconds)

Take a moment and notice your sanctuary. Notice any sounds that are here, in your sanctuary . . . If you were to inhale here, is there a scent in the air? When you look up, notice if you sense the sun, or perhaps clouds. You also may notice any wind, or a breeze on your face . . . And now, take a few moments and just *be* here and enjoy this place, your Inner Sanctuary. Let it fill your inner senses. (Wait about 20 seconds.)

And now, if you'd like, you can invite an Inner Guide to come be with you in your sanctuary . . . Your guide can show up as a person, an animal, a plant, or any *being*. Your guide will support you and answer any questions you have about your life.

So now, in the quiet of your own mind, send out an invitation for your Inner Guide to be with you here, in your Inner Sanctuary . . . Simply wait for them to arrive . . . And when they arrive, welcome them to your sanctuary. (Pause) And now, you can speak with your Guide as you would a good friend . . . If you'd like, talk with them about what you are here to shift or learn more about . . . You can ask your guide for any wisdom they may have about this topic in your life. Take a few moments and simply talk with your guide. (Wait about 60 seconds.)

And now, slowly move your awareness to your physical body . . . Notice if there is a place in your body where you typically feel your symptom. For example, if your symptom is depression, where do you feel the depression in your body? . . . Whatever your symptom is, notice where you sense it in your body. If you'd like, you can place your hand there.

And now, ask your deeper healing mind to show you one of the first times when you noticed *your symptom* . . . Just notice an earlier time when you felt your symptom and let the image of a younger self emerge in your awareness.

When you begin to sense a younger self, notice their age.

... And now, look around and notice *where* your younger self is—in other words, are they at home? If so, in what room? At school? If so, where in the building do you see them? ... Perhaps you can even get a sense of what your younger self is wearing ...

Does your younger self know that you, their capable adult self, is there with them? If you'd like, you can let them know you are there with them ...

Help them understand who you are—that you are their adult self, and that you've come to care for them and protect them ...

Notice what they are doing, what they are experiencing. Can you sense what your younger self is feeling right now? You can ask them ...

And now, see if you can notice their eyes ... Perhaps make some eye contact ... (Pause) If you'd like, ask your younger self what they need right now ...

Whatever they need right now, if you want to help them, go ahead and do that. (Pause)

And now, to provide maximum safety for your younger self, you can invite them to come be with you—in present time—where they will be safe, seen and cared for. If you want to invite this younger self to return home, with you, their adult self, go ahead and do that ...

And now, move your awareness to your physical body, and prepare a place in your body for them to live, to be present with you. Choose a place in your body where you will feel their youthful energy and presence . . . If you'd like, you can place your hand there.

And now, go ahead and invite your younger self to come be with you in present time. Invite them to come home. (Pause) *Sense* when they arrive there, with you, in present time. (Pause) When they arrive, welcome them *Home*. (Pause)

And now, just *be* with them. They may want to play, or rest, or just be with you. Take a few moments to establish a new relationship with this younger part of you . . .

And now, what sensations are you noticing in your body?

If you notice trembling or warmth or a sense of calm, this is a natural movement of your body's energy. If you'd like, let every cell be nourished with this healing sensation. See it filling your entire being . . .

And now, take a moment and thank your inner guide . . . Thank your younger self for joining you in present time. Notice you have moved them to a place of safety . . . Let them know they are always with you now. Their young energy has moved into present time with you, and they bring you many gifts.

And now, prepare to bring your awareness and your younger self slowly into your outer world.

In a moment, I will count up from 1 to 5. When you hear the number 5, you can then open your eyes, bringing your younger self into the outer world with you.

1 . . . beginning to be more aware of the room you are in.
. . . *2*, becoming more aware of your body . . . *3*, this is
when you slowly wiggle your fingers and toes–stretch, if
your body wants to stretch . . . *4*, taking a full breath . . .
and *FIVE* . . . When you are ready, slowly open your eyes,
feeling refreshed and awake.

Afterward:

Give yourself time to integrate the shift you just made in your
inner world. You may feel tired or want to dance. Maybe you
want to journal, or step outside and be in nature. Some people
are inspired to grab their paints and make art.

Acknowledge that you have just journeyed, wide-eyed, into
your helpful deeper mind, received new information, and
rescued the part of you that once was hidden and hurting. Now
that you have done this inner work, you have increased the
amount of energy running through your body!

*Be sure to read Chapter 8 so you know what to expect after working
with your SRI.*

The Invite to Write!
When we write, more information bubbles up from our
healing mind.

---

1. What were your thoughts when you read: "Yes, the event did happen. Yes, it is part of your history, but it is not located in the past. The emotional hook attached to it exists in present time." Write your thoughts here.

2. How does living the first seven years of life in the alpha/theta mind explain that your trauma is located in present time? Write your thoughts here.

3. At this juncture in your life, what will your day-to-day life look like after you deactivate your survival trances? What do you truly want to feel different as you move forward?

NOTES

*"Similar to a butterfly, I've gone through a metamorphosis,
been released from my dark cocoon, embraced my wings, and soared!"*

—*Dana Arcuri*

8

WHAT TO EXPECT AFTER DEACTIVATING YOUR SURVIVAL TRANCE

"Life will give you whatever experience is most helpful for the evolution of your consciousness."
—*Eckhart Tolle*

RELEASE AND REORGANIZATION

After you have done your inner work with one of the Self-Rescue Interventions, you will begin a period of integration known as Release and Reorganization. This is what your intelligent body automatically does to finish the healing process that your inner work initiated! You will likely have releases, all of which are described below. These releases are generally mild, even gentle.

As you move through these releases, your physical body reorganizes at the cellular level. When you brought your younger self to safety, you increased the level of energy in your body, and the cells happily adjusted to the new frequency! This is a natural response that happens when you deactivate your survival trance. Your alpha/theta levels of mind that had held the trauma for you will now complete the healing by orchestrating releases and then reorganizing at the cellular level.

Your release and reorganization can last a day, several days, or a week. The length of time depends on how much trauma you released during your Self-Rescue Intervention. For example, if you made a strong connection with that younger part of you, and if you rescued them from the danger they were in, you may have releases that last longer. And this is a good thing. When you consider how long you have suffered with the root of your trauma still in you, a few days of mild releases are a joy!

⇢↷↷ ✧ ↶↶⇠

Since we have many layers of fear in us, working with our traumatized younger selves isn't a "one and done" deal. Yet each time you work with the Self-Rescue Interventions, you shed one or more of those layers.

⇢↷↷ ✧ ↶↶⇠

THE MECHANICS

Here's how release and reorganization works in your body:

Each of our emotions has a unique electrical signature. For example, fear and anger vibrate in your body at lower frequencies. These sluggish vibrations cannot maintain healthy functioning at the cellular level. If fear becomes chronic, you are more vulnerable to mental and physical illness. These low frequency emotions cause your body to *contract*. Breath becomes shallow. Heart beats irregularly. Pulse is too fast.

On the other hand, emotions like, gratitude, love, and joy feel *expansive*. These emotions flood your body with a higher frequency that supports health in body and mind.

So, when you deactivate your survival trances, you switch from low to high frequency emotions. This raises the level of energy in your body and ignites releases in your *entire* being. Give your bodymind some time to reorganize on all levels of your being! This completes the healing process.

WHAT DO RELEASES LOOK LIKE?

Releases can show up on three levels:

1. Mental (Thought) Releases
2. Emotional Releases
3. Physical Releases

Old thoughts or emotions may pop in for a visit during your release and reorganization period. You may even notice some minor physical symptoms show up, such as congestion, flu-like symptoms, or ringing in the ears. This is a normal part of your healing experience. They are temporary and *will all disappear when you see clearly that they are just releases.* This, in fact, is your job—to realize these minor symptoms are *not* a sign you are coming down with something, but are just a release. This conscious act will wrap up this healing session.

⟶⟩⟩⟩ ⟡ ⟨⟨⟨⟵

Your job is to notice these minor symptoms are just a release! They are not a sign you are coming down with something.

⟶⟩⟩⟩ ⟡ ⟨⟨⟨⟵

DO YOU WANT TO SAVE THESE CHANGES?

A Software Analogy

When you're writing a document and forget to save the changes, your computer sends this prompt: *Do you want to save the changes to your document?*

A similar prompt from your body shows up as it busily reorganizes at the cellular level . . . *"Do you want to save these changes you made to your life?"* Assuming your answer is *"YES!"*, here's how you accomplish that: Each time you notice a release, tell yourself—out loud if possible—*"This is just a release!"* Don't buy into the idea that something is wrong. Give your bodymind time to reorganize on all levels! This is the action you can take to anchor the new changes in your life.

When you do this, your beta mind confirms with the alpha/theta mind that the new instructions are correct. This typically occurs a few times before the new operating system is firmly in place. This means your outer mind is recognizing and acknowledging the good work your inner mind is doing!

THREE TYPES OF RELEASES

1. Mental (Thought) Releases

Any thought that you change while in deeper mind may surface in your awareness later. For example, if you released self-hatred and switched to self-acceptance, the old operating system may check in with you, asking you to verify you want this change. If an old thought returns, say out loud, "Ah, you are just a release!" and send it on its way. Acknowledge the old thought is *just a release.*

2. Emotional Releases

An emotional release shows up when old emotions try to make a surprise visit. For example, let's say you release shame during your inner work, and it begins wiggling its way back into your life. Pause and remind yourself that *you authorized* the release of shame. Now it is your job to reinforce that change by saying aloud, *"THIS IS JUST A RELEASE."*

3. Physical Releases

Since the physical body is made of solid substance and is immersed in a field of energy, any change in the frequency can create a physical release. When we transmute old stagnant energies into more vibrancy, our body knows how to reorganize at the cellular level to accommodate the changes.

Common physical releases include congestion, soft trembling (especially in the core), ringing in ears, nausea, and even flu-like symptoms. Do not buy in to the idea that "something is wrong." Instead, these are only releases.

I have seen some clients have mild releases and others more potent. Depending on so many individual factors, each person experiences their own unique mix of releases. Some may have sniffles for a day, some ringing in the ears. Others may feel nauseous for a time. These and other temporary symptoms dissipate when you recognize your physical body is catching up with and integrating the inner changes you made.

When you anchor this in your awareness, the symptoms swiftly subside. The ill effects of your trauma dissolve.

The Invite to Write!
When we write, more information bubbles up from our healing mind.

---

1. Have you noticed any emotional releases after doing the Self-Rescue Intervention?

2. What about physical releases?

3. When you realized your symptoms were *just a release*, what shifted in you?

NOTES

A PERSONAL NOTE TO YOU, DEAR READER

I lay awake some nights thinking about how our species is beginning to shake off its collective trauma. We have struggled with our fears and frozen hearts since the beginning of time, and each generation continues to pass this turmoil on to the children. Life on earth, in a body, is hard to navigate—that's just the truth. Sometimes I think we come here as the innocent souls we are, and we engage in a life that has surprises and disappointments and hardships around every corner. A challenging game, indeed.

And this is where you, dear reader, enter my thoughts. It is you that inspires me and sparks my hope. Your inner work will end the repeating trauma in your lineage. This requires courage and bold action. You are on the leading edge of the cure!

Know this: Something is trying to awaken in you. You are finding ways to get to the root of your survival trances and let them out of the body. For some, this becomes a quest. Each of us who does our inner work and gets free, enhances the beauty of our collective humanity. I encourage you to follow what lights your spirit, and to live your life as a call to adventure. I wish you well on your journey!

—*Shuna*

ABOUT SHUNA MORELLI

Shuna Morelli, M.Ed. has developed the BodyMind Bridge™ System of Self-Recovery to reveal the astonishing ability of our deeper mind to help us heal. Shuna teaches a BodyMind Bridge Certification program and works privately with people wanting to heal from the survival trances that still disrupt their life. She has authored two other books: *What If Symptoms are Your Friend?* which serves as an introduction to BodyMind Bridge work, and *BodyMind Bridge and the Self-Healing Mind: A Guide for Therapists and the People They Serve.*

Connect with Shuna at www.shunamorelli.com

www.ingramcontent.com/pod-product-compliance
Lightning Source LLC
Chambersburg PA
CBHW020414130626
46549CB00006B/2564